£2

Pc

BRITAIN IN OLD   'HS

BIDEFORD

P A T   S L A D E

SUTTON PUBLISHING LIMITED

Sutton Publishing Limited
Phoenix Mill · Thrupp · Stroud
Gloucestershire · GL5 2BU

First published 1996

Cover photograph: en route to the County
Show, May 1907. Page 1: the statue of Charles
Kingsley.

British Library Cataloguing in Publication Data
A catalogue record for this book is available from the
British Library.

ISBN 0-7509-1155-7

Typeset in 10/12 Perpetua.
Typesetting and origination by
Sutton Publishing Limited.
Printed in Great Britain by
Ebenezer Baylis, Worcester.

To my grandchildren Richard and Zoë Slade

CONTENTS

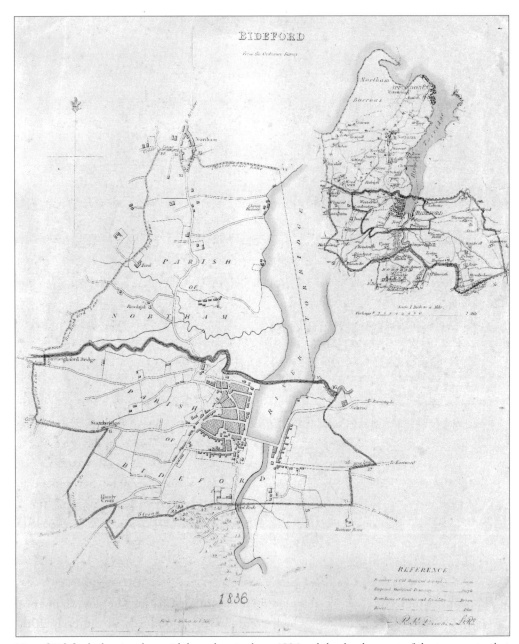

Map of Bideford, showing the parish boundary in about 1836 and the development of the town up to that time. The population figures taken from the census for the years between 1801 and 1981 show an increase of 9,223 people.

INTRODUCTION

It was with delight that I found the following extract in the *Bideford Gazette* for 1938:

100 YEARS AHEAD FROM THE MYTHICAL FILES OF THE BIDEFORD GAZETTE

Some readers say they regard the 50 & 25 year ago extracts among the most interesting items in this publication. History is interesting but, having got a crick in the neck through constant retrospect, a young correspondent who possesses a pretty wit has been indulging his fancy in a long view. 'Let us have a change' he writes, 'How about 100 years ahead?':

At a dinner held in the Municipal Reception Hall of Greater Bideford and Barnstaple, on Tuesday, the Mayor of Bideford gave some interesting reminiscences of his grandfather and quoted references from the *Bideford Gazette* in the course of a speech recalling the question of amalgamation between Bideford and Northam. He explained that Northam was a village standing on a rise above the estuary of the river and that Bideford a few miles up the river still had occasional maritime trade in those days. The coming of the North Devon Communal Grouping Act, he added, in 1988, marked a step of the utmost importance for the stretch from Lynton, Torrington and Hartland. An interesting point mentioned at a recent lecture to the North Devon Antiquarian Association was that Bideford and District used to be known as Kingsley's Country in honour of a certain Mr Charles Kingsley who wrote a novel entitled *Westward Ho!* which commanded a good sale in the early 20th century. A statue to Mr Kingsley used to stand at the end of Bideford Quay but it was destroyed by Air Raid in 1953.

Workmen excavating near what is still called the Broad Quay, despite its new classification as a number only, have discovered some remains of the Bridge that used to connect what was called East-the-Water with the west side of the river. It was known as the Long Bridge.

As a result of a collision between two helicopter planes competing in the slow-flying endurance race round Lundy, the Air Ministry have announced that any person flying at less than 100 m.p.h. will be liable to prosecution for loitering.

Among the items offered for sale by Messrs Blank, local interest centres around a 'wireless' set and amplifier stated to have been used at many fetes and by candidates under the old system of election in the district about 100 years ago. A primitive looking affair with valves and loudspeakers, it is to be placed in the local museum. A further addition to the museum was made last week when the Council of the Communal Group accepted with thanks the gift of a trombone once played in a Torrington Town Band. The instrument was discovered at the bottom of what used to be a coal-store. Coal-stores are still found in a few of the older houses.

Research into the history of Bideford in the last 100 years has been helped tremendously by old copies of the *Bideford Gazette*. The photographs help us to look back in time to see how Bideford has changed.

Development of Bideford included the widening of the quay and bridge, as well as the extension of the river bank by filling in the adjacent marshes. This enabled Victoria Park to be built, to celebrate Queen Victoria's jubilee in 1897. The coming of the railway made a marked impact on Bideford in 1855 and continued for nearly a century, finally closing in 1968. The smaller light railway from Bideford to Appledore, via Abbotsham, Cornborough and Westward Ho!, was never very successful and eventually closed in 1917. Road transport rose in popularity and carriage builders became garages and suppliers of fuel.

At various times there have been fifty-seven public houses in Bideford. Many have been closed for a long time, some have changed their names and a few are still the original pub mentioned in early directories.

Lack of space and/or illustrations prevent me from mentioning all of the churches, chapels and schools. Class photographs are fascinating and remind many people of the 'good old days'. I hope they will be continued in the future to preserve the past.

Pageants, carnivals, demonstrations and regattas were always well supported, but the organization of them must have caused many headaches.

I am indebted to the photographers of the past decades and to the producers of postcards. Especially I appreciate the people who, like me, don't throw their photographs away. Without these 'squirrels' there would be no pictorial records of the past.

AROUND AND ABOUT BIDEFORD

Old view of Bideford Bridge and town from East-the-Water, from an engraving dated 1831. This artist's impression of Bideford shows the town at a time when the west side had seen little development and the east side of the river even less.

Bideford's coat of arms. The grant of arms was made by the College of Heralds in 1936 as a gift to the town. In correct heraldic language the arms are blazoned thus:

> Argent over water barry wavy, in base a stone bridge of three arches proper masones, or, issuant from the centre arch an ancient ship the mast appearing behind the bridge also proper; on a chief gules three clarions or. And for the crest, on a wreath argent and azure an Elizabethan ship in full sail proper, the centre sail charged with a clarion or.

These bearings were devised from a combination of the Grenville arms and the old borough seal, on which is depicted the stern of what is probably a barge passing through an arch of the bridge. 'Proper' means in the usual colours, not heraldic ones. The bridge rises out of a silver and blue river. The Elizabethan ship of the crest (worn to distinguish the wearer, whose face would have been hidden by his iron helmet) was of course a tribute to Bideford's age-long connection with ship-building and the maritime trade. The headgear is an esquire's helmet. The Latin motto means 'Bold for King and Faith'.

Old Quay, mid-1800s. The quay has been widened on more than one occasion, the last time being in 1889/90. The principal part of the quay was the large open space in front of the Quay Gift Shop and was known as the Broad Quay. A tablet was placed here in 1931 to mark the old limits.

New Quay, early 1900s. In 1692 a new quay was constructed at the north end of the 1663 quay and extended to Bridgeland Street and the Potters Pill. (A Commission from the Court of Exchequer made 'the New Key built in the Port of Bideford, lawful.')

The site where the north end of Bideford Quay was situated in 1663. Steps of 10 feet wide descended to the river. The quay was 55 feet wide and extended 428 feet southwards to Conduit Lane. Bideford was a very busy port and needed a wider quay. This postcard, dating from the early 1900s, shows how it remained for many years after the previous widening.

On the quay, c. 1903/4. Various forms of transport are illustrated in this photograph. The train is waiting for passengers, while cargo has been unloaded from the vessel.

River bank, 1920. The route to Appledore by way of the river bank was pleasant, with majestic trees along the footpath through the woods known locally as 'the copse'.

River bank, 1920s. There were two cannons on each side of the park gates where children liked to play. In 1891, at a cost of £5,000, the promenade was constructed along the whole length of the quay. It was planted with trees to make a boulevard that enhanced the appearance of the lower part of the town.

Floods in the 1930s. Bideford Quay was flooded on more than one occasion. Sometimes the water would reach halfway up Bridgeland Street, especially on the left-hand side, sometimes as far as no. 30, and on the other side of the street above Warmington's garage.

The Swan Inn, Mill Street, 1950s. This is one of the pubs that no longer exists. It was situated at the end of Mill Street almost opposite Hart Street, and had a beautiful glass etched swan above its door.

PORT OF BIDEFORD AND KINGSLEY MEMORIALS, BIDEFORD

Port memorial, 1930s. Bideford lost its status as a port in 1886, but this was restored in 1928 and this memorial commemorates the occasion. Hetty Pym, the granddaughter of the builder, Mr Beer, presented the mayor with a silver trowel to mark the occasion.

Armada guns, just after the First World War. These guns stood outside the Bideford School of Art for years. They were believed to have been found in the sea and to date from the Armada. Various noteworthy experts have studied them and have said that they are definitely not as old as at first thought. They are no longer kept on the quay.

Bideford, Appledore and Westward Ho! Railway, *c.* 1910. A railway line had been suggested as early as 1866, but the company involved was wound up in 1870. Then a new company formed in 1896 and was contracted for the construction of the line, which was opened on 20 May 1901. Three Hunslet-built locomotives began operating on the line at this time.

Railway on Bideford Quay, *c.* 1910. The three engines were named *Kingsley, Grenville* and *Torridge.* As the trains passed through pedestrian areas, protective side plates were fitted over the wheels, and at a later stage 'cow-catchers' were fixed.

Railway terminus, 1903/4. The railway company wanted to extend the line and bring it nearer to the bridge, but many townspeople and the council objected. The company also faced the problem of the lack of a turntable. It employed navvies to dig up the road, but was so threatened that the excavations were soon filled in.

Railway route, 1903/4. The railway stretched from the quay and past the park along what is now Kingsley Road, crossing Northam Causeway and through the Kenwith Valley.

View of Bideford from the tower of St Mary's, 1890s. From this vantage point we can see across the bridge to the old ship-building yards at East-the-Water. To the far left is the Iron Church; the ceremony of laying the foundation stone of this church took place in October 1889. After St Peter's was consecrated it was dismantled and rebuilt in Ilfracombe.

Hogg's Corner, before 1903. The Hogg family set up business here as pharmacists at the beginning of the nineteenth century. In 1903 the buildings were demolished to make way for the new library.

Pill Bridge, looking from the river bank towards the quay, 1890s. This bridge crossed the Pill roughly opposite the present post office. The Pill was, as its name suggests, a small river flowing from the Kenwith Valley down towards the main river, following the route of the Kingsley Road.

Close-up of Pill Bridge, 1880s. The Pill ran into the River Torridge.

Ship moored at quayside, 1914. The SS *Devonia* traded from Bideford until at least the 1930s. As Bideford was such an important port, many vessels could be seen moored by the quay.

Public transport in the 1920s. Small buses owned by local firms, including Dymond's, picked up passengers on the quayside. The taxi rank was on the roadside.

Discharging cargo, 1890s. Ships were unloaded at the quayside using horse and cart. Sailing vessels carried all kinds of cargo, including coal, cement, lime and clay.

Unloading timber, 1930s. Steam ships replaced sailing vessels and began to bring in timber. Merchants such as E.W.S. Bartlett used horse-drawn wagons to take the timber to their yards.

Meddon Street (Maiden Street), 1910. This had some interesting buildings. The old Bideford Workhouse was built in 1835/6 and was operated by the Board of Guardians of the Poor. It was later called the Torridge Hospital. Other buildings in this street included a purpose-built hospital, which operated until 1925 (now Grenville Rest Home), and opposite was a field in which the parish pound was situated until about 1885.

Victoria Terrace, c. 1900. This terrace stands behind the market building. It was a favourite place for prospective parliamentary candidates to give their pre-election speeches.

General election meeting, Victoria Terrace, January 1910.
George Lambert and the Revd Mr Reed are addressing
crowds outside the market.

George Lambert (left), Radical, and the Revd Mr Reed on the same occasion.

Dingle's grocery store, Buttgarden Street, c. 1930. These people may be Mr and Mrs Dingle and their son. Mrs Dingle, the widow of Harry Dingle, died in Wales in 1946, aged 86 years.

Mr and Mrs Dingle and a shop assistant outside their store, c. 1930. Donald Dingle, son of Harry, is a director of Messrs Dingle & Co., the well-known Plymouth firm.

Entrance to Milton Place, Old Town, early 1900s. Originally this cul-de-sac would have been wide enough to provide access for the people who lived there. It led to Lansdowne Terrace, where in 1896 Miss Abbott started her private school for girls; this later moved to another location and finally became known as Westbank.

Entrance to Milton Place. The end house was partially demolished to make the approach to this street more accessible. Albert Place, on the right-hand side, escaped unscathed. The exact date of this photograph is unknown; it may have been taken in about 1916.

Fogaty's. This tobacconist/newsagent's shop at 7 Mill Street was owned by Mr Fogaty from the late 1920s to the end of the 1940s. Then it was sold to Nancekivell, who ran it for several years before selling it to Mr D. Watson (now trading in High Street). The large thermometer still hangs on the outside wall of the building.

Bridge Street, 1914. This must have been an important street in the early part of the nineteenth century. It was paved with cobbles and was the main road from the bridge to the top of the town and market. Until a relatively short while ago there were steps for the pedestrian at the top of the street.

Bridge Street, 1965. Note that the windows are masked. This preceded the demolition of this side of the street to provide more car-parking spaces. From the 'Slow' sign on the road it is clear that caution was needed to negotiate this steep hill.

Above: Bridge Street, 1930s. As we look down
the street we can imagine that at one time
there was two-way traffic. All of the buildings
on the left have now been demolished. Left:
Bridge Street, 1900. The railings on the left
were outside the chapel.

Van belonging to H.H. Burrow, radio engineer. In 1929, through the enterprise of this progressive firm, many local residents were for the first time able to see pictures, received by wireless at Bideford by means of a Fultograph.

Bideford railway station in the 1950s. The railway extension from Fremington to Cross Park was opened on 18 July 1855. The line was extended to Torrington in 1872. The final train ran in January 1983.

G.W. Fluck, *c.* 1915. This shop was a discount bookseller and fancy and commercial stationers at 15/16 High Street.

Bottom of High Street. This photograph from above Lloyds Bank, looking down to the quay, was probably taken just after the First World War. It shows a busy scene with the town scavenger (roadsweeper) in the middle of the road. Boyle's outfitters is on the corner of Allhalland Street.

Post office, High Street, 1918/19. The post office was opened for business in June 1886, and the 'increased convenience and comfort [were] felt and appreciated'. Prior to its opening, a notice was placed that January in the *Bideford Gazette* by the Trustees of the Long Bridge asking for tenders for constructing and fixing a new clock in the building. The competition was confined to silversmiths and clockmakers residing in the town of Bideford. Subsequently the tender by Mr Grimes of High Street (£42) was accepted and the clock was erected by public subscription. This post office was closed in 1959 when a new one was opened on the quay by the Lord Lieutenant of Devon, Lord Roborough. The new building cost £60,000.

Farleigh's stores. This large grocery business stood in High Street where New Look is situated. It was a grocer's in 1873, later a coffee tavern and the Kingsley Hotel before being owned by J.S. Farleigh in the early 1900s.

Looking up High Street, 1920. This interesting view of High Street shows the clock outside Truscott's, a jewellery shop, now J&A Cameras. Tiling on the front entrance step still bears the name of Truscott (and Squire).

Elliott & Sons, late 1920s. An announcement on 27 March 1928 in the local paper read: 'Special announcement – Elliotts moved to Kingsley Road from Bridgeland Street'. (See p. 113.)

Inside the spacious garage. On the right is one of the early lorries and at the back is Bideford's fire engine (one of the employees was the driver in the fire service).

Elliott & Sons, 1930s. This line-up of cars is in front of the salesroom.

Elliott & Sons, after the Second World War. A fleet of vans owned by Burrows of Bridge Street stands outside a modernized garage.

Royal Hotel, 1904 (above) and 1910 (below). In 1658 John Davies, a wealthy merchant, built himself a luxurious home by the riverside, close to the east end of the famous Long Bridge. The New London Inn stood next to the house, on the corner of the Barnstaple Road. In the 1880s Mr Stanley Heard combined the two buildings, and after much reconstruction it was opened in 1888 as the Royal Hotel.

Entrance hall, Royal Hotel, early 1900s. In the 1930s this hotel still had beautiful panelled rooms with their wonderful moulded ceilings.

Entrance hall, Royal Hotel, early 1920s. The beautiful staircase, about 200 years old, still remains, although the entrance lobby has changed a little.

Palm Court, Royal Hotel, early 1900s. This was once known as the Continental Courtyard. Along with a dining-room, hot and cold baths, and extensive stabling for four-in-hand coaches it provided a most 'Modern Hotel' in the west of England.

Palm Court, Royal Hotel, early 1920s. Once the courtyard of the house, it was later roofed in with glass, and a fountain set in the centre; the dining-room was formerly stables and warehouses.

Kingsley Room, Royal Hotel, 1920s. This beautifully panelled room is reputed to be where Charles Kingsley wrote a portion of his book *Westward Ho!*.

Tanton's Hotel, *c.* 1950. Several years ago this hotel was known as Chester's Commercial Hotel and it boasted that it had garages. An earlier picture shows a posting house on the premises and stagecoaches waiting outside.

Oak Room, New Inn, 1920. The New Inn is one of the oldest pubs in Bideford. At one time it had its own brewery, which used an underground stream flowing down Honestone Street and Bridge Street.

Dining-room, Vicary's Rooms, 1910–14. At one time owned by Vicary's, this room has been a skittle alley for a number of years. The building is now the Joiner's Arms, one of the many pubs that were around the market.

The Old Ship Tavern, 1910. This inn is reputed to be the site of the original 'Ship' in Charles Kingsley's book *Westward Ho!*, where the lovers of Rose Salterne dined together one market day and formed the Brotherhood of the Rose.

The Rose of Torridge, 1933. There was a disastrous fire in 1942 that threatened to destroy this building on the quay. Until recent years the inn was known as the Rose of Torridge, but it has also been known as the Blue Anchor, the Old Ship Tavern and the Newfoundland Hotel.

Rope Walk, *c.* 1912. Highlighting the changes in local manufacturing, J. Lewis May, author and native of Bideford, refers to the old Bideford rope-making industry, now long ceased, which was centred on the site still known as Rope Walk. He described it thus: 'At one end of the Strand was the entrance to what I suppose I must now prosaically call a long low-roofed shed but in those days it seemed to me as mysterious as the Sybil's cave. This was the Rope walk and thence, out of its cavernous mouth, there was wont to issue first a plodding patient horse, then a kind of wooden platform or land-going craft, on which stood two men, bearded and brawny, perpetually revolving a species of crank, or shaft, from which, by some mysterious means, they spun or seemed to spin as a spider spins its gossamer threads, an ever-lengthening tress of golden cable.'

The Torridge Inn, late 1920s. The names of publicans at the Torridge recorded in the directories of 1850 to 1935 are J.A. Houston, David Boys, John Henry Grant, Robert Grant, Philip Punchard, William Backway, Mrs Ann Backway, Charles Pope, Mrs Ann Pope, Richard Butler and Sidney Brunt.

Bideford Girls' Club, 1910. A senior resident of Bideford assures me that this club was in Coldharbour. A reference in the local paper mentions that at one time the club was held at a house on that street called 'Le Cotineau'. Earlier the club had met in Bridgeland Street. Mrs Thrupp was Honorary Secretary of the Girls' Club at one time. A Girls' Friendly Society was in existence in 1892.

Victoria Park, 1950s. This photograph shows a game of putting. In the background are the bandstand, shelter and old pumping station (now rebuilt as the tourist office).

Bowling Club, late 1940s. In November 1944 three suggested sites for a public bowling green were discussed by the General Purposes Committee of the council. The mayor (Alderman H.W. Fulford) visualized something bigger than just a bowling green – a civic sports centre incorporating a bowling green and other facilities. The decision was deferred until the layout of the playing fields had been agreed.

The Silver Ship. This was made in about 1750 and is inscribed: 'Presented to the Borough of Bideford by Sir Basil Peto M.P. in commemoration of the restoration to Bideford of the title and dignity of Port.' The model can be seen by appointment with the town clerk. It is 22 inches long and 24 inches high.

CHURCHES AND SCHOOLS

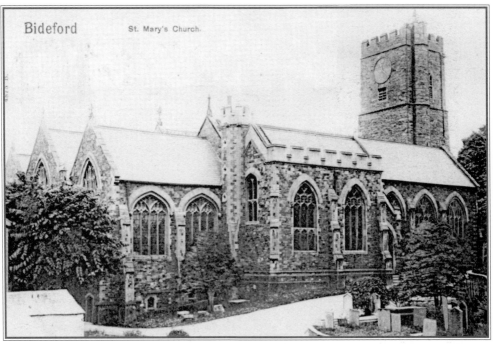

*St Mary's Church, 1906. The present church is the third to be built on the site. First the Saxons built one of
cob and wattle, very primitive by our standards. Then came the Normans, who were greater builders of
castles and churches. They left a legacy here of a fine church built in 1259. This was permitted to fall into
a serious state of disrepair. A decision was taken in favour of rebuilding rather than restoring, and most of it
was pulled down and a new church built in the early 1860s. The architect was Edward Ashworth and the
builder was E.M. White. The Norman tower and font were retained.*

The font at St Mary's Church. The fact that this font is circular makes it almost unique. Most of the Norman fonts (certainly the later ones) were square.

St Peter's Church, 1920s. Preceded by the Iron Church, St Peter's (East-the-Water) was built as a chapel of ease and consecrated on 28 June 1890 by the Bishop of Exeter. It was designed by Mr R.T. Hookway and the builder was Mr T.H. Glover of Abbotsham.

Church of the Sacred Heart, 1930s. Two rooms were rented in Bridgeland Street in 1882, and a priest came from Barnstaple. In 1892 the foundation stone was laid and the Church of the Sacred Heart was dedicated that December.

Lavington Chapel, 1938. This chapel has one of the most well-documented and interesting histories of local places of worship. In 1696 a site was leased from the Bridge Trust and a building erected called the Great Meeting House. The new chapel was built on the same site and opened in 1859.

Bridge Street Wesleyan Chapel, 1892/3. According to the Revd R. Granville, the original Wesleyan chapel in Bridge Street was built in 1815 and enlarged in 1854. The old chapel was turned into a Sunday School in 1892 and a new one was built. This was then demolished in 1969/70.

Bridge Street Wesleyan Chapel, 1940. A Bridge Street Methodist Anniversary report read: 'A Methodist Church had been erected on this site in 1813, and had been enlarged in 1831. In 1881 it was proposed to erect a new church facing on to Bridge Street. The memorial stones of the new building were laid in the spring of 1892 and the Church was opened on November 17th the same year. The Assembly Hall was opened in June 1893. On November 17th, 18th and 19th 1896 a Church Bazaar was held in the Music Hall, the magnificent sum of £714 being raised by this effort. In March 1899 the organ was opened, the service being taken by Silas Hocking, the novelist, and on Easter Monday of the same year there was a visit to the church by the Lord Mayor, Sir George Wyatt Truscott, Sheriffs, and several members of the London Common Council, through the instrumentality of Mr J.H. Lile. The Church was redecorated in 1911 and the Primary Hall opened in 1914.'

Approximately 2,000 people went to the church in May 1951 to listen to Billy Graham, the American evangelist. His words were relayed by land-line direct from the Harringay Arena, London. All the church accommodation was used and people queued outside the church door for an hour and a half before the relay service was due to commence.

The Bible Christian Chapel, 1910–14. This chapel was built in Silver Street in 1844. The original pastor was William Courtice. It closed with the opening of High Street Methodist Church in 1913/14 and was used as a glove factory until 1987, when the premises became a snooker hall. (See also p. 97.)

Children of what may have been Bideford's first kindergarten. Although I can find no records of a kindergarten in Bideford, I understand that there was one at Westbank in the 1920s. The background looks familiar, but with housing development it is difficult to pinpoint the location.

Church Junior School. Documents held in the Record Office (and now withdrawn) show that the building of an infants' school was proposed at Prout's Tenement, High Street, in 1845. This school closed in 1975 when the children moved to a new school in Chanters Road.

Entrance to Bideford Grammar School, 1935. In 1925 this site had been bought by Devon County Council and in 1928 further land was added, making a total of about 12 acres. Plans went ahead to build, but the world financial crisis postponed the construction until 1934, when the first turf was cut.

Bideford Grammar School, east quadrangle, 1935. The school 'was planned round two small grass-laid quadrangles. These are surrounded by cloisters into which open the various classrooms and other departments of the school.'

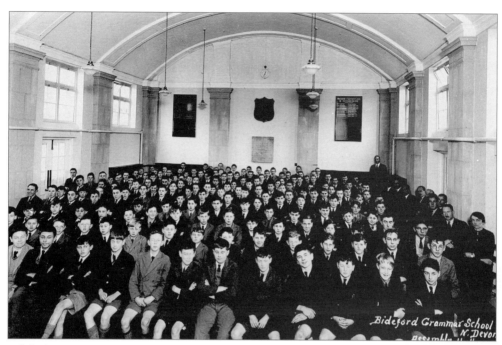

Bideford Grammar School assembly, 1935. The assembly hall is the central feature of the school. It is plain but dignified, with a barrel roof and a permanent stage. The boys in the front row include Bob Hockaday, Douglas Baker and John Harris (far left). The school was opened in the new premises at the beginning of the Christmas term 1935.

Bideford Grammar School crafts. The workshop for wood and metal work, containing a forge, electric lathe and a timber store, was in the west wing.

Bideford Grammar School pavilion, 1935. This site had been in use for some time as a sports ground. A subscription list was started for a pavilion, which was eventually opened in July 1934; at the same occasion Old Boys' Day was inaugurated.

Bideford Grammar School gymnasium, 1935. This was one of the finest features of the school, with adjoining changing room and medical room, projecting from the main block towards the west, where it formed one side of the playground.

Ursuline Convent, North Down Hill, *c.* 1915. The following was reported in the *Bideford Gazette* on 5 July 1904: 'A party of French nuns have taken North Down Hall, Bideford, which was for many years the Devonshire residence of Charles Kingsley. It is understood that they propose opening a school. From its grounds access can be obtained to the Roman Catholic Church.'

Ursuline Convent, *c.* 1915–18. 'On Wednesday a French ketch *La Francoise*, arrived at Bideford Quay from Port Aven (?) with a cargo of furniture, intended for the house.'

Ursuline Convent, 1917–20. When the nuns arrived they could not speak English and, being a closed order, they were not allowed to go out. They had a big black dog that was buried in the grounds when it died.

Stella Maris Convent, 1930s. In 1929 the Ursuline nuns left Bideford, and North Down Hall was acquired by the Sisters of Charity of Jesus and Mary, who changed the name of the convent to Stella Maris. The convent closed in 1996.

The opening ceremony at Geneva School, 1903. An extract from the school logbook reads: 'April 27th 1903'. Re-assembled this morning at the new Geneva School. May 8th 1903 Officially opened by the Mayor. School assembled at 10.30 and dismissed at 1 p.m. for the remainder of the day.'

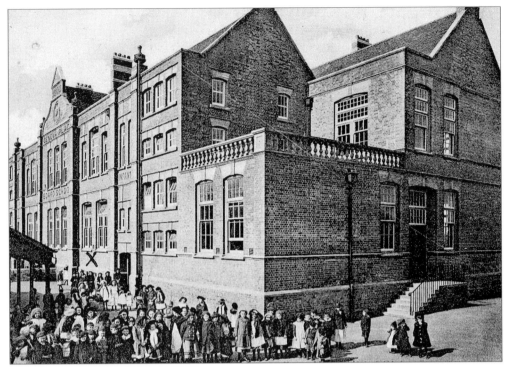

Geneva School, 1903. The school was originally built for infants and girls, but after the fire at the boys'
school in Old Town, the boys were transferred here. In 1892 an HMI report remarked that one hundred
infant children in the lowest class was very much overcrowded.

Church Infants' School, Class 4, 1916. In the second decade of this century these children were educated
at a school near the parish church of St Mary's. It was very small and later had a playground on the roof of
a building called the Church Institute.

Edgehill College, 1904 (above) and in the 1930s, after rebuilding (below). After the success of the nearby Shebbear College for Boys (about 15 miles from Bideford and still a boys' school today), a similar college with a Methodist foundation was approved for girls and in 1884 Edgehill College was established. Unfortunately, in 1920 a fire occurred and, although there was no loss of life, the building was destroyed. A new building opened in 1928.

Entrance to Edgehill College, 1930s. Students ('schoolgirls', as we were called) were forbidden to use this entrance. We were also forbidden to use the lower gate, having to walk to the top gate whatever the weather.

Edgehill College, assembly hall, 1920s. On VE Day in 1945 the whole school was assembled in the hall and Miss Hill, the headmistress, announced that the war in Europe was over. We sang the hymn 'Now thank we all our God' and were dismissed to have the rest of the day as a holiday.

The staff, Westbank School jubilee, 1946. This school officially opened on 21 January 1896 at 4 Lansdowne Terrace and the first pupil was entered at half term. A move to Enderleigh in Abbotsham Road in 1898 was followed by the move to Westbank in 1902.

Westbank School jubilee, 1946. The education of girls continued in this building until 1954, when the school finally moved to Sidmouth. It closed in 1971.

Westbank School, 1920s. In 1904 the *Bideford Gazette* reported that: 'It is interesting to note that this school had a small commencement about 8 years since. So great has been the increase in the number of pupils attending that about a year ago, the scholars had to be transferred from Enderleigh to new and commodious buildings – especially constructed – at West Bank. It is being carried on, on the High School principle, and if one can judge from the demonstration of the Swedish gymnastics, and the scholars' performance throughout Wednesday's entertainment, the school is under excellent management. Among its special classes, gymnastics play a prominent part, so that the body is well cultured as well as the mind.'

SECTION THREE

EVENTS AND CELEBRATIONS

The Lord Mayor of London, the Lady Mayoress, Mr Sheriff Badeley and the Mayor of Bideford (Mr H.R. Bazeley), Easter 1909. The Lord Mayor presented the cups to the winners in the BAAC marathon race. The prizes, valued at £20, included four silver cups, presented by Mr S.A. Miles of Chicago and Mr J.M. Lewis of Cardiff, plus three medals given by the club. The ten guinea cup was known as the Miles-Lewis Challenge Cup, and had to be won three times before being secured outright. The route was as follows: round the track in Victoria Park, past the art school, up Bridgeland Street, along North Road, up Raleigh to Silford, past Buckleigh, down to the Royal Hotel (Westward Ho!), along the top road through Northam, along the main road, then North Road, Mill Street, down Broad Quay past the Art School and one lap of the park.

'Welcome' arch, May 1907. Bideford welcomed its visitors to the Devon County Show by placing arches at strategic points on the route. The first to greet visitors was at the end of the bridge and was an evergreen structure with red lettering. The County Show had been held in Bideford in 1883, but the town has not hosted the event since the 1907 show.

'Success to the show', 1907. This arch was erected at Clovelly Road as the show was held at Moreton Park. A committee from the district, headed by the mayor (Mr J.M. Metherell), made extensive arrangements. Decorative arches across the streets and a profusion of flags and streamers greeted the thousands of visitors.

Double ceremony, 1906. The arch over the west end of the bridge together with the banner outside the library indicate that two ceremonies were taking place on the same day; in this case Mr C.S. Carnegie was opening the new library on behalf of Andrew Carnegie.

Unveiling ceremony at Kingsley statue, February 1906. The statue was of pure Sicilian marble, 8 feet high and standing on a massive pedestal of Portland stone 9 feet high. Charles Kingsley lived in Bideford for about fifteen months, and stayed for a time at both the Royal Hotel and North Down Hall. Both establishments claim that he wrote his book *Westward Ho!* while staying there. Based on Elizabethan times, the book has encouraged tourists, especially the Victorians, to visit the town.

Coronation celebrations, 1911. Two triumphal coronation arches were erected over the bridge, as well as one at the foot of High Street, bearing loyal and appropriate mottoes. The shops and private houses were also artistically decorated and the quay and bridge were dotted with fairy lamps, which made for a very picturesque scene.

Coronation arch, 1911. This was another arch built in traditional fashion to commemorate the coronation of the King. It stood across the High Street, a short way up from Allhalland Street.

Coronation church service, 1911. A commemoration service at St Mary's Church conducted by the rector (Revd T. Newton Leeke) was attended by the mayor and corporation, accompanied by the Bideford Band of the 6th Battalion Devon (Territorial) Regiment, plus members of the CLB, Bideford Boy Scouts and the fire brigade. Simultaneously a Free Church commemoration service was held in the Wesleyan church, the ministers of various Nonconformist denominations taking part. At each place of worship the service included 'O God our help in ages past' and the National Anthem. At the Church of the Sacred Heart, mass for King George was said at 8.00 a.m., and at 11.00 a.m. a solemn 'Te Deum' was sung. There was also a special early service at East-the-Water Church.

A very public luncheon, June 1911. A message on the reverse of this card tells all: 'As the Town Council made no arrangements at Bideford for anyone between the ages of 16 & 60 a few of us arranged a banquet on the quay between ourselves & made a grand day of it.' A quote from the *Bideford Gazette* reads: 'The spirit of celebration was very much in the air in Bideford during June 11th, on the occasion of the Coronation of His late Majesty King George V and memories of the jollifications on that occasion will no doubt be recalled by this photograph.' At the market a free luncheon was given to all residents over sixty years of age, but a number of the younger generation decided to arrange their own festive luncheon. Catering was provided by the Steam Packet Hotel on the quay and the laden tables were erected on the riverside of the quay. The many faces in the photograph include Mr E. Woodyatt, Mr Charlie Morris, Mr S. Parkhouse, Mr R. Prance, Mr S. Priscott and Mr W. Goodenough. For this special occasion a one-man band was present (right). Moored against the quay was a Danish merchant ship, the captain and mate of which were invited to take part in the celebration. Later in the afternoon the party moved off to Westward Ho!, where the jollifications were continued.

New gates, Victoria Park, 1912. The main gates of this park were presented by the late George Oliver Peard in memory of his wife. The smaller gates were erected by the town council to commemorate the coronation of King George V.

Opening of the new gates, 9 November 1912. After its enclosure the park was formally opened by the mayor, Cllr W.T. Goaman JP. The entrance gates are of wrought iron and in the centre of each is a bronze copy of the borough coat of arms enclosed in a scroll.

Lifeboat arriving at Bideford railway goods yard, May 1910. The *Jane Hannah McDonald* arrived at the goods yard by rail in May, but the ceremonial launch was postponed until September that year because of the death of King Edward.

Launch off the quay. There were several launches off the quay, when the lifeboat dropped from 4 to 5 feet into the water, but when the *Jane Hannah McDonald* was launched the drop from the carriage until the boat struck the water was more than 10 feet – beyond the experience of even the oldest lifeboatmen.

Lifeboat curtsy. At a given signal the men hauled on the ropes with a will and the lifeboat, 'shooting' with a graceful gliding motion off the carriage, struck the water with a beautiful splash and rose buoyantly after the shock.

Lifeboat being rowed down river. The usual way to deliver the new lifeboats was to launch them off the quay and then either sail or row down to Appledore. The *Robert and Catherine* was launched in a similar fashion in June 1912.

Demonstrations on the quayside, 1910. The weather was somewhat unkind but the launch of the lifeboat was combined on this occasion with the regatta, and crowds watched the lifeboatmen demonstrate the various skills that could be put to good use on a rescue exercise. The display took place at the Broad Quay (now called Jubilee Square). There would have been a full grandstand on the quayside, with entrance and seats by ticket only. A local report read: 'The speeches were brief and to the point and yet covered all the good, while the particular references to the local lifeboat crews were particularly appropriate and encouraging. The ceremony altogether and particularly the religious portion of it will long be remembered by all who were privileged to take part in it.'

Meeting on the quay, *c.* 1915/16. As the crowd consisted mainly of women with only a few men to be seen, this could be a meeting to encourage support, possibly financial, to help the wartime activities.

Devon Yeomanry/Hussars on the bridge, 1908. Local troops in the Devon Yeomanry and Hussars from around the area gathered at East-the-Water and paraded through Bideford on their way to Northam Burrows for their annual camp. On the reverse of this card the results of their polo match had been sent to a friend.

Mustering at Bideford, early part of the First World War. The Royal North Devon Yeomanry are thought to be signing up new volunteers. Men mustered from Torrington and Bideford then went to Barnstaple. Names of men enlisting can be found in the *Bideford Gazette* for the early war years.

Horses at Bideford Market. This card was sent to Canada from Bideford and besides the usual greetings it read: 'Today should have been our Regatta Day but owing to the war it has had to be postponed.' The card was posted on 19 August 1914.

Forget-Me-Not Day, August 1915. 'Madam Jessie Strathearn ARAM, the well known vocalist from London, who has been on a visit to Bideford, before leaving by the noon train today, will at 11 o'clock sing a popular song in the Pannier Market and afterwards from the New Inn balcony, on behalf of the "Forget-me-not" Day appeal for support to the County Fund organized by the Mayoress of Exeter for providing tea and sandwiches, cigarettes etc to the troops as they pass through Exeter on their way to the front. The Mayoress of Bideford assisted by the ladies and the Bideford Girl Guides are undertaking the sale of "Forget-me-nots". The Wesleyan Band will give a concert in aid of the fund in Bideford Park tomorrow (Wednesday) at 7.30 p.m.'

Track laying prior to a railway locomotive leaving Bideford, 1917. A reverse shunt was required into Bridge End Street so that the locomotive could be taken across the bridge.

Locomotive across the bridge. Hundreds of people watched the train go across the bridge on its journey to help the war effort.

The Meet, 22 January 1909. There were several hunting appointments advertised in the *Bideford Gazette* in this year. These included the Devon and Somerset Staghounds, Mr Scott Browne's hounds, plus the Eggesford, Stevenstone and Exmoor Hounds.

The Meet, 1909. This started from outside the Royal Hotel. One of the earliest references to hunting dates from 1867 when Capt. Willett, on retiring, sent his acknowledgements to landowners and farmers over whose land he had hunted.

The Meet, 1911. In the late 1890s the Cheriton Otter Hounds met outside the Royal Hotel with Joe Cheriton in charge.

The Meet, March 1911. 'A large number of Bidefordians gathered at East-the-Water end of the Long Bridge yesterday morning to witness a meet of the Stevenstone Hounds. It was a fine bright morning after storms in the night.' Capt. and Mrs Wood were there.

Heard's outing, *c.* 1930. On 5 July 1938 it was reported in the *Bideford Gazette* that '32 members of Heard Bros. Staff went on a most enjoyable outing to Plymouth on Saturday June 25th. The outing was arranged by Heard Bros. Social Club and the party left Bideford by motor coach proceeding by way of Torrington to Plymouth. While the party was at lunch, a telegram was received from the directors, who were unable to be present through indisposition.' Mr B.V. Braund was the vice-chairman of the social club and Mr R.J. Backway was the secretary.

SS *Hubbastone*, October 1920. The launching of the first steel ship to be built at Bideford was a great occasion. The SS *Hubbastone* of 1,150 tons was built at Hansen's Shipyard at Cleavehouses.

SS *Hubbastone*. Hansen's Shipyard was in operation from 1919 to 1924. It apparently started from a game of golf at Westward Ho! golf links where men often talked business after a game of golf; as a result of one such conversation Bideford got its shipyard.

Parade on the quay, 1930s. Parades of all kinds crossed the quay led by the town band. The carnival had, in the past, raised funds for the hospital and was always well supported.

Carnival parade on the quay, 1930s. Carnivals have long been a tradition in Bideford and many of the local shops and businesses, such as Chope's, Heywood's, Trapnell's and Boyle's entered floats. Maj. Tyreman of Abbotsham always led the procession riding his horse.

Lorry falls from the Long Bridge. This accident made an unusual subject for a postcard. It happened on 4 February 1924 when a heavily laden oil lorry, displacing about 25 yards of the temporary iron and wire railings, toppled over the side of the bridge and crashed down on to the sparlings and river bed 25 feet below. The driver, Mr Charles Cloke, aged 48, was seriously injured. The passenger, the son of the driver, had abrasions to his forehead and over one eye, but after treatment at the hospital was allowed to go home. The accident happened during the process of widening the bridge, the roadway having been temporarily narrowed at that part where the works were in progress, and the permanent parapet had been replaced with wire railings. The vehicle was loaded at that time with 300 gallons of oil and forty 2-gallon cans of petrol.

Another shot of the lorry. Mr Cloke worked for the Anglo-American Oil Co. Various people had heard the crash and described it as being like the report of a gun. Even PC Broad, who was just sitting down to dinner at the police station, rushed out to the balcony to see what had happened. Mr Charles Henry Northcote, brother of Mr Fred Northcote (the Barnstaple district representative of the Anglo-American Oil Co.), was cycling across the bridge. He had noticed the lorry approaching but, momentarily distracted, he looked ahead again to find that the lorry had disappeared and at the same time he heard the crash. When he realized what had happened he cycled off to fetch a doctor. Mr Cloke survived and lived for a further nine years.

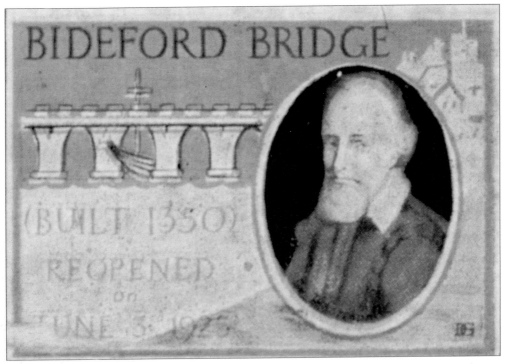

Postcard detail. This commemorated the reopening of the bridge, after its widening, on 13 June 1925. Celebrations also took place to mark the occasion.

Banner parade. On the reverse of this postcard it reads: 'This is a snapshot taken on the Broad Quay during the election. See if you can recognize your father. G.J.' The name on one of the banners was G. Borwick, who stood as parliamentary candidate for Barnstaple in 1910.

Collapse of the Long Bridge, 1968. On the evening of 9 January 1968, Mrs V. Brogden and Mrs M. Bowden, while crossing the bridge, heard a noise and saw masonry falling into the river. They reported what they saw on a 999 call and the bridge was closed to all traffic. A temporary tubular footbridge was. erected the following day, but meanwhile a ferry service using Army DUKWs helped to transport people from east to west and vice versa. Emergency services were planned because the bridge carried a high-pressure gas main, a water main and six telephone cables. The bridge was opened to light traffic in April and proposals were made to widen the carriageway (from 16 feet to 18 feet) by reducing the footpaths. In September 1968 it was reported that repair work would be completed by the end of 1969, but a high-level bridge could not be erected for a number of years.

Scout's funeral, April 1912. The death of a young Bideford Scout, Robert James Alford, aged 17 years, occurred suddenly on Easter Monday 8 April 1912. It was reported that large crowds lined the route to the Higher Public Cemetery for his funeral.

Bideford Band, Bideford Park, 1920s. Members here include, back row: Mr Day sr, ? Jewell, Bernard Branch, Mr Goaman?, Mr W. Cole. Front row: Mr Bobby Day, Mr Heal (eventually bandmaster).

Building Kingsley Road, 1925. The new route used part of the track of the old Bideford–Appledore railway route. The roadway was staked out and work helped to absorb some of the local unemployed men.

Workmen, Kingsley Road, 1925. The Ministry of Transport approved acceptance by the council of the tender of Messrs Smethurst of Oldham for the construction of the alternative loop on the Bideford–Northam Road at £20,002.

Excavating for Kingsley Road, 1925. The road connected the River Pill with the Bideford–Northam Road at Raleigh Cross, where the level of the old road had to be raised 3 feet to avoid what would have been a very awkward junction.

Filling in the marsh, 1925. The stone filling (obtained from Mr Fulford's quarry on the road opposite) was laid in the marsh in 2-foot layers, each one rolled by a 10-ton roller.

Kingsley Road nearing completion. The road was opened on 6 June 1927 at a total cost of £30,000, which included £200 for setting back the Kingsley statue and £500 for the drainage of the Pill. A line of pennies, the naming of a Bideford and District fire engine and a grand pageant completed the ceremony.

D.F.B. Stucley, c. 1910. Launched in 1908, this boat was bought for £40 complete. A committee was formed to collect shillings from local working men. The boat was ordered from Sims of Putney.

Regatta Day, 1951. The Sea Cadets' launch *The Revenge* was moored at the East-the-Water side of the river for the regatta. BAAC came third in the novice fours for the Orr Ewing Challenge Cup. The crew were M. Griffiths (stroke), E. Giddy, G. Cawsey, J. Bowden and J. Harris (cox).

Regatta Day, 1897. As early as 1857 the description of the regatta included donkey and pony racing on the sandbanks at low tide.

Regatta Day, 1897. That year there were 'confectionery and refreshment standings, booths of acrobats, penny peeps and organs, rifling for nuts, well-furnished marquees, and a band of musicians stationed to enliven the multitude who pace to and fro four feet deep. Donkey racing and duck hunting continued at low water.'

Rainbow Pageant, May 1935. Directed by Mr C.S.F. Harding, children from seven local schools met in the sports ground arrayed in dresses of many shades of the rainbow representing twenty-one parts of the British Empire. The daughter of the mayor and mayoress, Cllr and Mrs W.E. Ellis, was dressed at Britannia.

Maypole dancing, May 1935. Children from local schools entertained their parents and friends with maypole dancing in the park. Dancing was organized after the pageant with Bideford Band playing the music.

Coronation parade, 1937. Bideford Town Silver Band, wearing their new uniforms, head the procession to Victoria Park for a united service. Immediately behind the band came 'A' Company 6th Devons under 2nd-Lt G. Oerton, followed by V.A.D. Devon under the commandant, Mrs Symes.

Coronation proclamation, 1937. The mayor (Mr Goaman) and corporation assembled at the bandstand in Bideford Park to present an address. The rector read the call to worship and the invocation. A hymn was followed by the lesson, read by the Revd A.E.J. Cosson.

Borough of Bideford
Coronation Celebrations, 1937

HISTORICAL PAGEANT

Sports Ground, Bideford

Wednesday, May 12th, 1937

Procession commences at
2.30 p.m.

•

Thursday, 13th May, 1937
Repeat Performance at 6.30 p.m.

Characters and Names of Performers - Price 2d.

Pageant programme, 1937. This contains the names of participants in a total of eight episodes connected with Bideford's history, plus the names of the twenty-five members of the town band and fourteen people who represented local historical celebrities, including Charles Kingsley, Sir Francis Drake and Rudyard Kipling; they all took part in a grand march past.

Pageant march past, 1927. The pageant procession of about five hundred performers assembled at the East-the-Water end of the bridge. Those dressed up are, left to right: Mr S. Mules (as Amyas Leigh), Mrs Braund (Mrs Leigh) and Miss L. Robertson (Ayacanora).

Pageant in the sports ground, 1927. This was part of the march past, which comprised people dressed as 'The Rulers of our Seas, Canadian Mounted Police, India' and many others.

Pageant, 1927. A giant historical pageant was held to celebrate the opening of the Kingsley Road. These ladies of the court were, left to right: Mrs S. Elliott, Miss Preece, Miss Margaret Morris (Singhalese lady), Miss Mary Helps (Burmese lady) and Miss M. Lock (attendant).

Ship arrival, 1937. *The City of the True Cross*, a captured Spanish galleon, featured in the pageants of 1927 and 1937. Mr W. Jordan of Westward Ho! was the designer and 'articifer' of the craft, helped by Mr W. Harris, Mr F. Harris and staff at Messrs P.K. Harris.

Demolition of Bridge Street, with Boyles Cycle shop on the right, 1969. This was not a particularly good time for the residents of some of the streets in Bideford. Pimlico Place and Providence Row were demolished in 1968 and part of Bridge Street was demolished in 1969.

Demolition of Bridge Street. On 6 June 1969 it was reported in the *Bideford Gazette* that 'demolition work is proceeding in a section of Bridge Street on the left (downhill) from the former Methodist Church to the junction with Allhalland Street'. It was planned to provide car parking on the site.

Mill Street works, late 1940s or early 1950s. Work commenced at the end of Mill Street. A resident in Bridgeland Street remembers that the sewage pipe main drains were the first group, then gas, followed by electricity and finally the water. Each time the road was dug up then, after completion of that work, refilled. This continued all the way down Bridgeland Street. To get to the shops people had to walk over steel plates and the chaos continued for months.

Coronation celebrations at the Glove Factory in 1937 (above) and, probably, 1953 (below). Annie Jeffrey (née White) from Appledore is sitting third from the left in the top photograph. The workroom was well decorated with garlands and flags on both occasions. The factory closed as Sudbury's Glove Factory and is now a snooker hall. (See also p. 48.)

Parade outside Edgehill College, May 1943. Members of local Girl Guide companies lined up outside Edgehill College to greet and form a guard of honour for the visit of Chief Guide Lady Baden Powell.

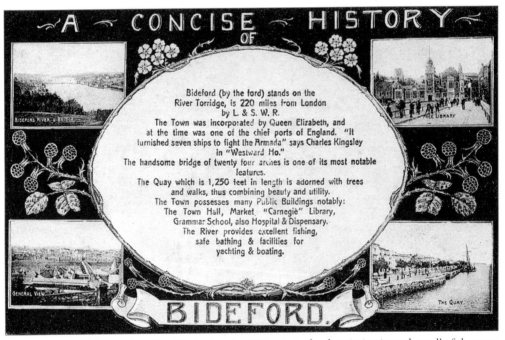

A CONCISE HISTORY OF

Bideford (by the ford) stands on the River Torridge, is 220 miles from London by L. & S. W. R.

The Town was incorporated by Queen Elizabeth, and at the time was one of the chief ports of England. "It furnished seven ships to fight the Armada" says Charles Kingsley in "Westward Ho."

The handsome bridge of twenty four arches is one of its most notable features.

The Quay which is 1,250 feet in length is adorned with trees and walks, thus combining beauty and utility.

The Town possesses many Public Buildings notably: The Town Hall, Market, "Carnegie" Library, Grammar School, also Hospital & Dispensary.

The River provides excellent fishing, safe bathing & facilities for yachting & boating.

BIDEFORD.

Concise history. This card describes Bideford in the 1920s. A similar description is on the wall of the town hall facing the bridge. It would be interesting to design a card for today and include some of the modern-day attributes of Bideford.

JUST PEOPLE

Visit of Lady Baden Powell to Edgehill College, 5 March 1943. Lady Baden Powell is standing (centre) at the main entrance to the college with, left to right: Mrs Reeve (Divisional commissioner), the Revd R. Pyke (School Bursar), Mrs Pyke, Miss E. Cuthbertson Hill (Headmistress) and Lady Clinton (County Commissioner). Lady Baden Powell briefly toured Devon, visiting Bideford and Torrington on this Friday.

A. Ellis, lacemakers, 47 Mill Street, 1900. To the left of the lace shop was the entrance to young Miss Ellis's grandfather's builder's yard. Her father later took the business on. It was Ellis & Son who rebuilt Edgehill College after the fire there in 1920. On the right of the lace shop was an outfitter's shop belonging to Miss Ellis's uncle. This is now a butcher's shop. Pictured here are Miss Ellis's grandmother (the owner of the lace shop) and cousin Winnie. The grandmother didn't use her hands for housework or cooking because they were 'too precious', so her niece, Winnie, kept house. The old lady received lace from other workers as well as making it herself. She often sewed pieces together to make patterns and stoles. She won a first prize at the exhibition at Crystal Palace for her work.

Westbank Preparatory schoolchildren, 1963. These children were in the transition department of the school after its move to Sidmouth.

Westbank Preparatory School, 27 July 1954. Back row, left to right: Carole Braddick, Gillian Holland, Hilary Dawe, Geraldine Lee, Sara King, Anne Abell. Second row: Jane Bierbaum, Christine Andrew, Nancy Gorrell, Hilary Barron, Susan Heard. Third row: Dina Webber, Julie Wilmott, Joanne Banham, Jennifer Vipond, Susan Hutchins, Mary Lambert Gorwyn, Jill Frith. Front row: Jane Walters, Kate Thornton, Diana Milner Brown, Jane Hartnoll, Anita Fursey.

Westbank Preparatory School, summer 1951.
Left to right: Nancy Gorrell, Joanna Tope,
Carole Braddick.

Bridgeland House Parents National Educational Union (PNEU) School, 13 July 1928. Back row, left to right: -?-, ? Pickard, Winnie Strudwick, Gwen Cleverdon, Eric Mitchell?, Dot Adams, -?-. Middle row: -?-, Winsome Fulford, -?-, Trevor Slade, ? Ashplant, -?-, Joan Hopson, -?-. Front row: Joyce Pickard?, -?-, ?Fulford, -?-, -?-, ? Taylor.

Church Lads Brigade, 1947/8. Back row, left to right: -?-, Derek Bidgway, -?-. Second row: -?-, Gerald Cloutman, Bob Kelly, Paul Pope, Eric Giddy, Brian Rogers, Michael Bonetta. Front row: Gerald Adams, Peter Adams, the Revd Derwent Davies (padre), Mr Pope, Tom Holloway, Rodney Beer, Bobby Cluett.

Bideford Grammar School, 1947/8. Back row, left to right: Jack Colwill, Rodney Lee, Derek Mounce, Brian Rogers, Tony Down, Lionel Cork, ? Bartlett, John Wadey, 'Nobby' Clarke, Ernie Stoneman, Charlie Davis, ? Harding. Second row: Michael Bonetta, Lionel Green, 'Oiseaux' Bird, David Montague, -?-, Eric Giddy, ? Coster, Ted Hatswell, John Jewell, Peter Loughlin, Peter Adams. Front row: ? Stapleton, ? Waldron, ? Lee, Desmond Bennett, Sam Jeffries, Reg Reed, John Harvey, Richard Cornelius, David Yelland, John Manley, Peter Colwill.

Presentation of coronation mugs, Geneva School, 1937. Back row, left to right: Ivor Wakeley, Ray Sawtell, Basil Pidgeon, Gerald Trick, Fred Tovey?, Cyril Ebsworthy, David Salisbury, Cyril Gullick. Second row: Jack Mitchell, Donald Grant, Fred Jeffery, Jack Holloway, Jack Prouse, Trevor Gubb, -?-. Front row: Studley Shute, Bobbie Hooper, Tommy Giddy, Douglas Copp.

Presentation of coronation mugs, Geneva School, 1937. Back row, left to right: Ivor Wakeley, Dolly Griffiths, -?-, Joyce Huxtable, Christine Copp, Barbara Harding, Connie Harris, -?-, Betty Young, Basil Pidgeon, Ray Sawtell, -?-, Jack Holloway. Second row: Jack Mitchell, Donald Grant, Bobbie Hooper, Eileen French, Fred Jeffery, Fred Tovey?, -?-, Doris Salisbury, Trevor Gubb. Third row: Cyril Gullick, -?-, -?-, Studley Shute, Freda Bissett, -?-, -?-, Mavis Cornish, Barbara Daniel, Douglas Copp, Gerald Trick. Front row: Cyril Ebsworthy, Enid Elston, Jean Ackland, Jean Roberts, Edna Prust, Joan Dark, Esme England, Jack Prouse.

Geneva School, 1925. Back row, left to right: Ken Eagles, Bill Jeffery, Fred Mounce, Eric Watkinson, Fred Tithecott, Cyril Cole, Jim Little, ? Witton, ? Richardson, ? Richards. Second row: Bert Squires, Wilf Stapleton, Clarrie Rogers, Len Randall, Garfield Williams, Cyril Challis, John Lee, Harry Moore, Gordon Edwards, Bill Mills, John Prust. Third row: Ken Summers, ? Bond, ? Wrey, ? Sherborne, Mr George King, Frank Sanders, Bill Watts, ? Scoines, Ernie Comer, ? Kelly, Sid Cole. Front row: Stan Short, ? Palmer, ? Way, ? Jewell, Joe Heard, ? Baker, Ken Harvey, Andrew Tucker.

Bideford Amateur Rowing Club, winners of the Orr Ewing Challenge Cup at Bideford Regatta, 1905. Back row, left to right: Bill Blackmore, Ned Madge, J. Blackmore, A. Lake (stroke). Front row: Fred Stephens (captain), B. Lake (cox), H.N.G. Stucley (president).

Bideford Amateur Athletics Club marathon race, April 1909. The Lord Mayor of London, Mr Sheriff Baddeley, presented the prizes to the following competitors: Winners (1) T. Whitlock, (2) G. Herniman, (3) E. Pierson, (4) W. Prance, (5) W. Puddicombe, (6) C. Dipstale, (7) A. Shute, (8) S. Bowden.

Bideford hockey team, 1930/1. Back row, left to right: Wilf Stapleton, Dick Yeo, Cyril Braund, ? Smale, Ken Braund. Middle row: Gordon Hill, ? Marshall, Jack Cowie, Roy Ellis, Sammy Heywood, Percy Wadey. Front row: Joe Glover.

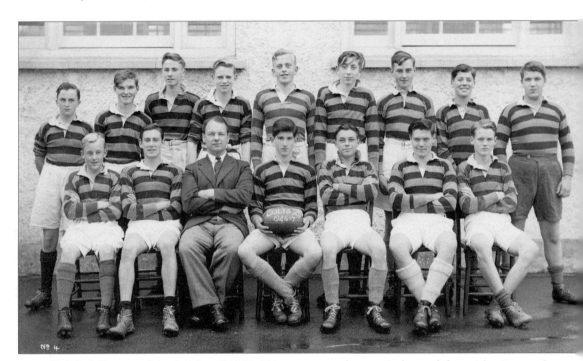

Bideford Grammar School Colts, 1946/7. This team was unbeaten. Back row, left to right: Desmond Bennett, ? Waldron, -?-, ? Prosser, -?-, ? Stoneman, ? Johnston, Kenny Beer, Dennis Harding. Front row: Peter Loughlin, Michael Bonetta, Mr Hewlett, Tom Bonetta, Rodney Beer, Eric Giddy, Michael Goss.

Bideford Grammar School 1st XV, 1947/8. Back row, left to right: Lionel Green, Philip Fulford, Ernie Stoneman, Alan White, Lionel Cork, Dave Montague, Peter Heath, Eric Giddy, Brian Rogers. Front row: Peter Loughlin, Michael Bonetta, Mr Gerald Norman ('Duke'), 'Oiseaux' Bird, ? Doherty, Charles Mill, -?-.

Bideford RFC 1st XV, 1950/1. Back row, left to right: Bill Lock, Arthur Lee, Ray Sawtell, Bob Colwill, M. Woolf, -?-, A. Hoare, T. Bonetta, -?-, N. Trickey, M. Bird, -?-, T. Sawtell. Front row: B. Lesslie, R. Bird, J. Little, R. Jones, E. Slade, B. Beer, E. Giddy, C. Mills, C. Davies, Gerald Woolf.

The Revd J.B. Stedeford, the Revd W.B. Reed and E.J. Soares MP outside the Three Tuns inn, Bideford Quay, *c.* 1910. This public house was until recently the South West Gas offices.

Right: Mr George Giddy, mace bearer, *c.* 1905. In May 1906 George Giddy sent in his resignation of the office of mace bearer, as a result of ill health, after having held the post for twenty years. He mentioned that he had acted as tything man and had held other public offices for forty years, having served under three different town clerks. Below: Cannons outside the park gates, 1922. This was a favourite playing place for these four boys. They also used to play ball around this area. Left to right: -?-, ? Broomhall, Wilf Stapleton, Len Stapleton.

ELLIOTT, Bridgeland Street, BIDEFORD, Devon

Carriage Builder and Motor Engineer.

'Phone I Y 2.   Telegrams : 'Elliott's Motors, Bideford.

Advertisement for Elliotts (now Warmington's Garage) in Bridgeland Street. The proprietor, W.H. Elliott, is standing outside. The photograph was probably taken in about 1903–5.

Employees of Elliott's Garage, *c.* 1907. Back row, left to right: W.H. Elliott, Bill Squires (joiner), Bill Glover (smith), R.S. Elliott, Ned Bond (painter), Jimmy Jenkins (wheels and tyres), Arthur Woodcock, Harry Heard (engineer), William Elliott. Front row: -?-, Arnold Harding (metalwork).

Inside Elliott's Garage. Those present include Mr Elliott, Mr Bond, Jesse Shortridge, Jimmy Jenkins, Bill Squires, Bert Elliott (aged 15), Bill Glover, Bruce Woodcock, Harry Heard, Stan Elliott (aged 14) and Arnold Harding. Until a very short time ago the staircase was still in the workshop of Warmington's.

Demonstration drive for Elliott's Garage, probably in the early 1900s. H.W. Elliott is driving, with Miss W.O. Elliott in the back seat. The aim was to show that the car could be chauffeur driven.

Staff of Elliott's Garage, *c.* 1924/5. Left to right: Ernie Renshawe (foreman, who also drove the fire engine), Bob Hearn (salesman), Len Stapleton (who worked for five years for 7*s* 6*d* per week to learn his trade), Arthur Kelly, Bill Tucker (salesman).

Southern National Riverside Works, 1929. Back row: left to right: Charlie Piper, Leonard Jeffries, ? Green, Bill Major, Percy Bright, ? Smith, ? Little, Leslie Symes, ? Manning, Ron Parker. Second row: Jack Wrigley, Sam Lewis, Bill Garnsey, Louis Waldron, -?-, Harold Sellick, Sammy Dinacombe, Fred Baker, -?-, 'Bronco' Branch, Philip Labbett, Tommy Shute, Bill Banbury, Harry Prouse, Malcolm England, -?-, A. Harris. Third row: Sid Easterbrook, Harry?, ? England, Jack Marshall, ? Morgan, Norman Webber, -?-, Jack Frayne, Bill Norris. Front row: 'Farmer' Hookway, Bill Ward, Alf Budd, ? Wills, Oliver Hart, -?-, ? Backway, ? Matthews.

Horse and caravan on the quay. This postcard was sent to a shop in Torrington with the following message on the reverse: 'With the compliments of the Caravan Touring Company Ltd. (W.F.).' The caravan is parked outside where Bideford post office is now situated.

The end of the bridge, 1870. Behind the bridge is the shop of Mr and Mrs James Berry. Mr Berry was a basket maker and ham smoker. The Berrys are standing in the doorway of their shop. On the left can be seen part of the Old Grammar School, which was removed from this site in 1879. Mr Berry's shop was cleared away to make room for the Bridge Buildings.

Green's china shop, High Street, 1887. This shop belonged to Mr George Green, and is now Lloyds Bank. A Mr George Green was living there in 1891, aged 54. On 14 April 1891 it was announced that: 'The Devon and Cornwall Banking Co. have purchased the premises of Mr G. Green in High Street.'

East-the-Water (Coronation or Jubilee 1935/7?) Committee. Back row, left to right: -?-, Mr B. Beer, Mr Tom Taylor, Mr Fred Hookway. (Mr F. Kivell is standing behind in the peaked cap.) Front row: Mrs Causey, Mrs Bowden, Mrs Johns, -?-, -?-.

Torrington Street, East-the-Water, *c.* 1935/7. Back row, left to right: Mrs Johns, Mrs Tucker, Mrs Blackmore, Doris Braunton, Mrs Blackmore, Joyce Schillers, Mrs Schillers, Mrs Hart, Mrs Beer, Mrs Evans. Front row: Mrs Pym, Mrs Bowden, Mrs Pam Shortridge, Katy Shortridge, Mrs Bromell, Mrs Hearn, -?-, Mrs Freda Bird, Mrs Lamey.

East-the-Water Radios Dance Band, *c.* 1936/7. Back row, left to right: Mr B. Beer, Mr Hocking, Mrs Knight, Mr and Mrs Ellis, Jean Bonetta, Mrs Shortridge, Mrs Turner, Emma Hearn, Doreen Tithecott, Mr Tom Taylor. Second row: Hetty Pym, -?-, -?-, -?-, Mr and Mrs Beer, Mrs Kivell, -?-, -?-, -?-, -?-, Mr Turner? Third row: Marjorie Taylor, -?-, Mrs Evans with Bobby Evans, Gladys Taylor with Pam Taylor, Mrs Hearn, John Lee, Audrey Beer, Mrs F. Bird with Jill Bird, -?-, Mrs Pym, Mrs Morris. Front row: Rona Hearn, Patsy Pym, Pam Shortridge, Mrs Shortridge, Marie Lester, Barbara Morrish, Michael Bonetta, Marion Bonetta, -?-.

Torridge Street, *c.* 1935/7. Those present include, standing, left to right: Mrs Johns, Mr Tom Taylor, Mrs Geary, Mrs Prouse, Gladys Spearman, ? Braunton, Joyce Knight, Margaret Tucker, Margaret Mills, Lily Tithecott, Muriel Braunton. Standing, right: Derek Shortridge, Gladys Taylor, Roy Causey, Cyril Braunton. Sitting, left: Mr Squire, Stan Kivell, John Brown, ? Tithecott/Sherborne, Cyril Lamey. Sitting, right: Mrs Geary, Mrs Tucker, Mr B. Beer.

Jubilee party at Torrington Street, 1935. Those present include, standing, left: Mrs Bowden, -?-, Mrs Lamey, Jean Bonetta, Mrs Dolly Evans, Mrs F. Bird, Jill Bird, Mrs Pym. Second row (children) -?-, -?-, -?-, Margaret Hookway, -?-, Norman Glover, Anita Glover, Cyril Lamey, -?-, -?-, -?-, Mrs Schillers, Beryl Braunton. Third row, sitting: Cllr and Mrs Ellis, Mayor and Mayoress of Bideford. The boy who stands out, top right, is Derek Shortridge.

Jubilee party in the school playground, East-the-Water, 1935. The photograph includes, far left, Mr Turner (the cobbler, sitting on the bench, turned towards the camera), Mr Tom Taylor (at the back). Standing, left: Dolly Evans, Bobby Evans, Mrs Shortridge. Sitting, left: Pam Shortridge, Donald Spearman, Philip Evans, Graham Evans, Joyce Knight, Doreen Harding, Lilian Harding, Hetty Pym, -?-, -?-, -?-, -?-, -?-. Standing, back: -?-, Mrs Pym, -?-, -?-, -?-, -?-. Sitting: Jean Bonetta, Marie Lester, Patsy Pym, -?-, Barbara Morrish, Emma Hearn, Michael Blackmore, Claudine Blackmore, Valerie Hearn, Doreen Tithecott. Standing, right: Marjorie Taylor, Gladys Taylor, -?-, Freda Bird, Jill Bird.

Adults in the school playground, East-the-Water, 1935. Standing, left: Dolly Evans, Gladys Taylor, Freda Bird. Sitting, left: Cllr and Mrs Ellis, Mr Hocking, -?-, -?-, -?-, -?-, -?-, Mayor and Mayoress Goaman, Mr Little. Sitting, right: -?-, Mr and Mrs Turner, -?-, Mr and Mrs Beer, -?-, -?-, -?-, Mr Billy Beer. Standing, back: Mrs Knight, Mrs Shortridge, Mrs Hearn, Mrs Pym, Mrs Kivell, Mrs Morrish, Marjorie Taylor. Sitting, far right: Doreen Harding, Hettie Pym, Lilian Harding.

The Rector of Bideford, the Revd Mr Manning, in the grand procession of the pageant, 1937. Mr Manning, who was at St Mary's Church from 1921 to 1946, is dressed as Bishop Bronescombe, who dedicated the church after its rebuilding.

The Little family displaying some of their ware in the early 1900s. This family ran a china and hardware business from Elm Grove.

HRH Prince Philip inspects the Bideford Naval Cadets in Park Avenue, 1952. The mayor, Mrs Cox, looks on. Those present in the front row include Albert Keen and CPO Bobby Nicholls. The officer in front is Mr Chubb. Also in the photograph are Basil Bloyce, Lewis Ellis, and Jimmy Nicholls.

Bideford Naval Cadets march past at the visit of Prince Philip.

ACKNOWLEDGEMENTS

I should like to thank the following for the loan of photographs: Mr and Mrs T. Bird, Mrs Dorothy Cleaver, Mrs Gwen Cleverdon, Mr and Mrs E. Giddy, Miss L. Keen, Mr B. Pidgeon and Mr Wilf Stapleton; for permission to reproduce copies from their collections: Messrs Knights (Photographers Barnstaple), A. Littlejohns, and Mr C. Barfett; and NDRO, North Devon Athenaeum, and the *North Devon Gazette and Advertiser*. Also, a special thank you goes to Mike Davy, Bob Fancourt, and all of my friends and colleagues at the Bideford and District Community Archive for the proofreading, comments and encouragement. I should like to thank all who have helped with identifying and naming people.

Finally, I should like to thank my husband, Edgar, for his forbearance while this book has been in preparation.

Every effort has been made to trace the owners of copyright material.

Lincoln
Lincoln Cathedral
The Lincolnshire Coast
Liverpool
Around Llandudno
Around Lochaber
Theatrical London
Around Louth
The Lower Fal Estuary
Lowestoft
Luton
Lympne Airfield
Lytham St Annes
Maidenhead
Around Maidenhead
Around Malvern
Manchester
Manchester Road & Rail
Mansfield
Marlborough: A Second Selection
Marylebone & Paddington
Around Matlock
Melton Mowbray
Around Melksham
The Mendips
Merton & Morden
Middlesbrough
Midsomer Norton & Radstock
Around Mildenhall
Milton Keynes
Minehead
Monmouth & the River Wye
The Nadder Valley
Newark
Around Newark
Newbury
Newport, Isle of Wight
The Norfolk Broads
Norfolk at War
North Fylde
North Lambeth
North Walsham & District
Northallerton
Northampton
Around Norwich
Nottingham 1944 74
The Changing Face of Nottingham
Victorian Nottingham
Nottingham Yesterday & Today
Nuneaton
Around Oakham
Ormskirk & District
Otley & District
Oxford: The University
Oxford Yesterday & Today
Oxfordshire Railways: A Second
   Selection
Oxfordshire at School
Around Padstow
Pattingham & Wombourne

Penwith
Penzance & Newlyn
Around Pershore
Around Plymouth
Poole
Portsmouth
Poulton-le-Fylde
Preston
Prestwich
Pudsey
Radcliffe
RAF Chivenor
RAF Cosford
RAF Hawkinge
RAF Manston
RAF Manston: A Second Selection
RAF St Mawgan
RAF Tangmere
Ramsgate & Thanet Life
Reading
Reading: A Second Selection
Redditch & the Needle District
Redditch: A Second Selection
Richmond, Surrey
Rickmansworth
Around Ripley
The River Soar
Romney Marsh
Romney Marsh: A Second
   Selection
Rossendale
Around Rotherham
Rugby
Around Rugeley
Ruislip
Around Ryde
St Albans
St Andrews
Salford
Salisbury
Salisbury: A Second Selection
Salisbury: A Third Selection
Around Salisbury
Sandhurst & Crowthorne
Sandown & Shanklin
Sandwich
Scarborough
Scunthorpe
Seaton, Lyme Regis & Axminster
Around Seaton & Sidmouth
Sedgley & District
The Severn Vale
Sherwood Forest
Shrewsbury
Shrewsbury: A Second Selection
Shropshire Railways
Skegness
Around Skegness
Skipton & the Dales
Around Slough

Smethwick
Somerton & Langport
Southampton
Southend-on-Sea
Southport
Southwark
Southwell
Southwold to Aldeburgh
Stafford
Around Stafford
Staffordshire Railways
Around Staveley
Stepney
Stevenage
The History of Stilton Cheese
Stoke-on-Trent
Stoke Newington
Stonehouse to Painswick
Around Stony Stratford
Around Stony Stratford: A Second
   Selection
Stowmarket
Streatham
Stroud & the Five Valleys
Stroud & the Five Valleys: A
   Second Selection
Stroud's Golden Valley
The Stroudwater and Thames &
   Severn Canals
The Stroudwater and Thames &
   Severn Canals: A Second
   Selection
Suffolk at Work
Suffolk at Work: A Second
   Selection
The Heart of Suffolk
Sunderland
Sutton
Swansea
Swindon: A Third Selection
Swindon: A Fifth Selection
Around Tamworth
Taunton
Around Taunton
Teesdale
Teesdale: A Second Selection
Tenbury Wells
Around Tettenhall & Codshall
Tewkesbury & the Vale of
   Gloucester
Thame to Watlington
Around Thatcham
Around Thirsk
Thornbury to Berkeley
Tipton
Around Tonbridge
Trowbridge
Around Truro
TT Races
Tunbridge Wells

Tunbridge Wells: A Second
   Selection
Twickenham
Uley, Dursley & Cam
The Upper Fal
The Upper Tywi Valley
Uxbridge, Hillingdon & Cowley
The Vale of Belvoir
The Vale of Conway
Ventnor
Wakefield
Wallingford
Walsall
Waltham Abbey
Wandsworth at War
Wantage, Faringdon & the Vale
   Villages
Around Warwick
Weardale
Weardale: A Second Selection
Wednesbury
Wells
Welshpool
West Bromwich
West Wight
Weston-super-Mare
Around Weston-super-Mare
Weymouth & Portland
Around Wheatley
Around Whetstone
Whitchurch to Market Drayton
Around Whitstable
Wigton & the Solway Plain
Willesden
Around Wilton
Wimbledon
Around Windsor
Wingham, Addisham &
   Littlebourne
Wisbech
Witham & District
Witney
Around Witney
The Witney District
Wokingham
Around Woodbridge
Around Woodstock
Woolwich
Woolwich Royal Arsenal
Around Wootton Bassett,
   Cricklade & Purton
Worcester
Worcester in a Day
Around Worcester
Worcestershire at Work
Around Worthing
Wotton-under-Edge to Chipping
   Sodbury
Wymondham & Attleborough
The Yorkshire Wolds

To order any of these titles please telephone our distributor, Littlehampton Book Services, on 01903 721596
For a catalogue of these and our other titles please ring Regina Schinner on 01453 731114

BRITAIN IN OLD PHOTOGRAPHS